Peoples and Nations
of
Europe

A short history of each country in Europe

Sheila Fairfield

YOUNG LIBRARY

Peoples and Nations

Peoples and Nations of **Africa**
Peoples and Nations of **The Americas**
Peoples and Nations of **Asia**
Peoples and Nations of **Europe**
Peoples and Nations of **The Far East and Pacific**

First published in 1985 by
Young Library Ltd
International Press Centre
76 Shoe Lane, London EC4A 3JB

ISBN 0 946003 47 5

Printed and bound in Italy

Designed by Behram Kapadia
Maps by Mark Wojcicki
Picture research by Sara Steel

A note on the entries

All nation states and dependencies have an entry, although those for dependencies are much briefer. Each entry for a nation state is accompanied by a map, while those for dependencies refer to a map elsewhere in the book which shows their position. Places which are part of a country, but which are geographically separated from the main area, do not have a separate entry but are referred to in that country's entry. There are countries mentioned in this book which do not have an entry of their own here, but in another volume of the 'Peoples and Nations' series; the index includes a reference to the volumes in which entries for those countries are to be found.

CONTENTS

Albania 58

Andorra 26

Austria 56

Azores 11

Belgium 6

Bulgaria 28

Channel Islands 52

Cyprus 32

Czechoslovakia 36

Denmark 50

Faeroes 34

Finland 8

France 20

Germany 30

Gibraltar 60

Greece 38

Holland 15

Hungary 53

Iceland 59

Ireland 10

Isle of Man 51

Italy 12

Liechtenstein 9

Luxembourg 23

Malta 49

Monaco 49

Norway 19

Poland 17

Portugal 54

Romania 34

San Marino 60

Spain 4

Sweden 26

Switzerland 42

United Kingdom 44

Yugoslavia 24

Glossary 62

Index 63

SPAIN

Spain is a high, rocky country, cut off from the rest of Europe by a range of mountains called the Pyrenees. There is little fertile soil. Central Spain has bitterly cold winters and hot, dry summers. The most prosperous parts have always been along the east and south coasts (by the Mediterranean Sea) and along the north coast (by the Atlantic Ocean).

Before 1600 B.C. there were rich cities in the south and east. The people mined precious metal and traded across the Mediterranean. The Phoenicians (who came from Lebanon) came to trade before 800 B.C. They founded Cadiz. The Greeks came after 600 B.C., not only trading but settling. Greek farmers brought the first olive trees and the first grape vines. Afterwards came the Carthaginians from north Africa, who founded Cartageno.

The Mediterranean coast became a mixture of original Spaniards, Phoenicians, Africans, and Greeks. Inland it was different. Celtic tribes had crossed the mountains from France on to the bleak, central plateau. There, and in the north, they lived as shepherds. In the north-east were the Basque people, living as sailors, fishermen and small farmers. They spoke an ancient language unlike any of their neighbours' speech.

In 206 B.C. the Romans took Spain into their empire. However, they did not master the country for 200 years. There were many risings and wars. The fiercest rebels were the Lusitanians who lived in what is now Portugal. Roman Spain became rich and civilized, but it always depended on tightly controlling the people.

The empire ended. The Roman Catholic church survived as the central power in Spain. The church kept the empire's ideas on the need for control.

In A.D. 711 Spain was invaded by Moslems from North Africa. They ruled southern Spain. The Catholic rulers whom they pushed out went north, and settled with their followers in Asturias.

Under the Moslems (called Moors) southern Spain had cities, arts, and learning better than any in Europe. Many Spaniards became Moslem, although the Moors did not make them do so. Southern Spain became a mixture again: Moors, Christians, Mozarabs (Christian Spaniards living in Moorish areas), Moriscos (Moors converted to Christianity), and Mudejars (Moslems living in Christian areas).

There were few people living in the centre. After a time the northerners moved down into it, taking more and more of the thin pasture for their herds. Then they built castles to protect themselves; the central land was called Castile, from the Spanish word for 'castle'. They grew strong enough to attack

4

the Moors.

By 1248 all Moorish Spain had been conquered except Granada (which went on until 1492). There were then several Catholic kingdoms. By 1469 Castile and its neighbour Aragon had swallowed all the others, except Navarre in the north-east. In that year, Castile and Aragon were united when their king and queen married. In 1516 all Spain was ruled by one Catholic king.

The new country won a great empire, mainly in America, and became powerful in Europe too. Spain was then so important that the Spanish Catholic church would not put up with anyone who disagreed with it.

Then in 1700 a French prince came to the Spanish throne. French kings ruled until 1807. The common people disliked the 'frenchified' life of the rich; they began to glorify everything traditionally Spanish. The parts of Spain which were once kingdoms disliked the central rule of the French kings; they kept trying to break away.

During the nineteenth century the link with France was ended, but the empire was lost. All sorts of arguments broke out. Some wanted a powerful king and a powerful church. Some wanted a republic, and hated the church. Some thought the army should rule. Some wanted a strong central government, and some wanted the old kingdoms to have more freedom. All these arguments at last broke out in a civil war, in 1936.

After the war, Spain had a republic under General Franco until 1975, when it became a kingdom again. The Catholic church stopped

The beautiful Court of Lions is in the Alhambra, the palace built near Cordoba by the Moorish kings who occupied southern Spain for centuries.

being the official religion in 1978. Some of the regions, especially the Basque country in the north-east, would still like to be independent.

Spain includes the Balearic Islands (Majorca, Minorca, and Ibiza) which lie in the Mediterranean Sea.

BELGIUM

The land now called Belgium used to belong to the Belgae, a fierce tribe of Celts. In 57 B.C. the Romans defeated them in battle. The Celts and their land were taken into the Roman empire. The Romans then had to defend the land against other tribes from east of the Rhine. By A.D. 400 they had allowed one of these tribes, the Franks, to live in it; they knew that the Franks would keep the others out.

There were then two kinds of Belgians. Celts had got used to a Roman way of life and spoke a language like early French. Franks had a northern way of life and their language was like Dutch. When the Roman empire ended the Franks built up an empire in its place.

There were many local rulers, each in charge of a small state, and the emperor was their overlord. By about A.D. 800 the emperor's rule was weak. Viking pirates raided the country and he could not fight them off. The local rulers had to do it on their own. When they had succeeded, they wanted more freedom, because they knew they could look after themselves.

There were also towns learning to be independent. The Franks had become Christian, and merchants could travel about safely. There were many cargo ships on the River Scheldt, and rich trading towns nearby.

On the left you see a lady making lace in the traditional manner. Bruges, in Flanders, has been a leading lace-making town for hundreds of years.

This lively picture shows a market in Antwerp in the sixteenth century. By this time Antwerp had grown to be the commercial capital of Europe.

Ghent, Bruges, Antwerp, and Liège were all important.

The Frankish empire split in two in 843. After that the Western Frank (or French) kings and the Eastern Frank (or German) kings competed for control of 'the Low Countries' (the area we now call Belgium and Holland). Both found it difficult. The rich towns and small states almost ruled themselves. The most important of the states was Flanders.

Some time after the year 1000 the population suddenly increased. With less room for farming, Flanders stopped keeping sheep; instead it bought wool from England, made it into cloth, and sold it back. People set up small workshops where they made goods for sale. Trade was better than ever, and the people were soon experts in handling money. Many became bankers.

Still, on either side of them, were the French and German rulers. Each wanted to be able to tax these rich people. Each also felt that he would be safer if their land, which was flat and easy to invade, belonged to him.

The Germans – the Hapsburg family – became overlords in 1482. They ruled Austria and many German states. In 1516 they also became kings of Spain.

In 1598 the northern part of the Low Countries rebelled against the Hapsburgs; it became Holland, an independent country. The southern part did not fight so hard against the Hapsburg emperor, and he was able to keep it. This was mainly because the people, unlike the people of Holland, still

7

shared the Hapsburgs' Catholic religion.

From then on there were invasions whenever there was trouble between the Hapsburgs, the French, and the Dutch. The Dutch took the land around the mouth of the River Scheldt, and stopped Belgian ships using it.

In 1815 it was decided that neither the Hapsburgs nor the French should have Belgium. The country was united with Holland under a Dutch king. The Belgians hated it. In 1830 they rebelled, and between 1831 and 1839 Belgium was accepted as a new country.

The people have been invaded twice since 1900, but they have kept their industries and their prosperity. Belgium is still a crowded place, with two kinds of people and two languages. The Flemings speak a kind of Dutch and the Walloons in the south speak French.

FINLAND

Finland is a low-lying country of forests and lakes. There are few big towns, and they are all in the south. In the north are the people called Lapps, who live by keeping herds of reindeer.

The Finnish people themselves are thought to have come from around the Volga River, in what is now Russia. Finland has a long frontier with Russia, and relations with Russia have always been important. Finland also has a long coast on the Baltic Sea, looking across to its other important neighbour, Sweden.

Finland is a cold country with long winters.

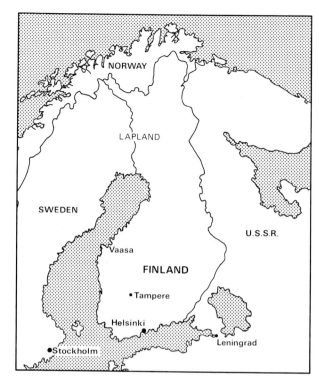

There has never been much good land. The early Finns lived on small farms where they had to work very hard to stay alive. They became very tough, but even so there were times when many died of hunger. Young men left Finland to work as soldiers in foreign armies.

The Swedes conquered Finland in the fourteenth century. In many ways the country did well under Swedish rule: farming improved, timber and a kind of tar from the forests were exported. At the same time the Swedish language and Swedish customs were brought in. The Finns accepted this for so long as the Swedes protected them from Russian invasion.

There were many wars between Sweden and Russia, and the Finns were in the middle. They suffered greatly. Russia conquered Finland in 1808 and held it until the First

World War of 1914–18.

In 1917 there was a revolution in Russia. The new communist government agreed that Finland should be independent. Then there was civil war in Finland, as Finnish communists saw their chance for a revolution in Finland too. The communists were defeated with German help.

In 1939 there was a quarrel with Russia and a Russian invasion. Then Finland, with Germany, was involved in the Second World War. When the war ended in 1945, Finland was given new frontiers; some land in the north and east went to Russia, and Finland became the shape it is today. There are Finns, Lapps, Swedes, and Russians living in modern Finland; Finnish and Swedish are both official languages.

LIECHTENSTEIN

The people of Liechtenstein speak German and are descended from German ancestors. In the Middle Ages, when Germany was made up of many small states, there was a tiny state called Vaduz which belonged to Count Hartmann III. By 1434 it had reached its present size, which is still only about 62 square miles (160 square kilometres). Unlike other German states, Vaduz did not become part of modern Germany. Instead it became the Principality of Liechtenstein, which it still is. The town of Vaduz is the capital. (See map of Germany)

Most of the country is composed of forests, lakes, and islands, requiring numerous bridges and causeways.

IRELAND

Ireland is an island divided into two states. Most of it is the Republic of Ireland (or Eire, in Irish). The north-eastern corner is Northern Ireland, which is part of the United Kingdom.

Celtic tribes arrived in Ireland before 300 B.C. Small kingdoms developed, under one High King, who ruled at Tara. The Irish Celts became Christian after A.D. 400; Irish monasteries became important, but the faith did not last everywhere.

After 800 there were raids by Danish and Norwegian pirates, called Vikings. The Vikings were traders as well as raiders; they founded Dublin and other Irish towns as trading stations.

By 1100 there were four kingdoms – Ulster, Munster, Leinster, and Connaught. There was no longer a strong king with overall power. The people lived in tribes or clans, each with its own chief and living on its own land. The tribes had frequent fights with the Viking towns, and raided the coasts of Britain for slaves.

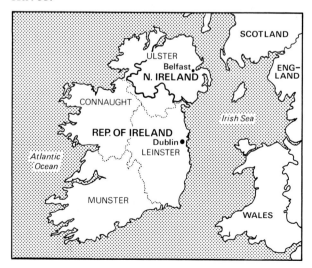

The English king wanted to invade Ireland and bring it under his own control; his chance came in 1169. Dermot, King of Leinster, asked him for help against an enemy. English knights were sent to Ireland, but they used Dermot's war to win Leinster and Munster for the English king.

For centuries the main diet of the Irish poor was potatoes. When the harvests failed in the 1840s there was famine, and a huge migration to the U.S.A.

The English were not strong enough to conquer all Ireland, and the Irish were not strong enough to drive them out. Two very different nations began trying to share the island. The English lands were held by warlords who were as savage as the Celts; there were frequent wars.

In the sixteenth century the English conquered the rest of Ireland. They began to impose English law, language, and religion. England had become Protestant during the sixteenth century; Ireland had a mixture of Catholic Christianity and older, Celtic beliefs. This conquest was as much resented by the warlords as by the Irish.

Rebellions were put down. English and Scottish settlers came to farm the land, and to live by English law and the Protestant religion. New laws made things easy for them and difficult for non-Protestants.

By the eighteenth century the most powerful people were Protestants of Scottish and English descent. Most Catholics were peasants, and poor. The main crop for peasant farmers was the potato.

There were more rebellions, and these did bring about change. The anti-Catholic laws were altered in 1829. But in 1845 a disease began to kill the potato plants, and a famine began in southern Ireland.

Many people died; others left Ireland for England and America. Most of those who stayed believed that English rule did not work, and should end. But ideas of the future varied a lot, and there were bitter arguments.

Most of Ireland became independent in 1921, as the Irish Free State (later called the Republic of Ireland). There was still fighting; some wanted to keep a link with England, some did not.

Ireland's support of the Catholic James II led to their defeat by William III at the Battle of the Boyne.

Northern Ireland did not join the new state. The people there had escaped the famine and were fairly prosperous. They were mainly of British descent, and chose self-government within the United Kingdom. Irish Catholics living in Northern Ireland were not happy with this. The arguments turned into riots in 1969, and there has been violence ever since.

AZORES

The Azores is a group of islands in the north Atlantic, west of Portugal. They were found by sailors from Portugal, and Portuguese settlers followed. The islands have belonged to Portugal since 1840.

ITALY

Italy stretches from the Alps right down into the Mediterranean Sea. It includes the islands of Sicily and Sardinia. Most of the country is a peninsula, with the Appenine mountains running down the middle. The good land is in the valley of the Po river, in the north, and in small areas around the coast. South Italy is particularly rocky, dry, and difficult to farm. The north has always been the richest part, and the most go-ahead.

From about 800 B.C. the people of the north were the Etruscans. No one is sure where they came from, and no one has yet translated their language. They lived in cities, from which they traded across the Mediterranean.

Further south, on the plain of Latium, lived the Latin people who first used the Latin language. Also to the south was the city of Rome, founded in 735 B.C. by Latin-speaking people. Further inland were the Samnites, who lived in the mountains.

In the far south, and in Sicily, there were colonies of settlers from Greece.

After about 400 B.C. the people of Rome

became more powerful than their neighbours. By 275 B.C. they had control of all other Italian people. Roman government and the Latin language spread everywhere.

Romans were clever, practical, and well-organized. They had a well-trained army and a good civil service. Roman Italy had many cities, rich farms, and all sorts of trade. The Romans built an empire which spread all round the Mediterranean, across Europe to the Rhine and Danube rivers, and across the English Channel into Britain. In A.D. 395 this enormous empire was halved between two rulers. Rome became the capital of the western half.

Marco Polo leaves Venice in 1271 for his great journey of discovery through Asia. At that time Venice was the busiest port in the world.

The fourth-century Roman emperor Constantine was converted to Christianity. The medieval painting on the right shows him being baptised.

There had never been enough Roman – or even Italian – soldiers to keep the huge empire under control. The emperors had got used to using warriors from all over Europe. These men were either subjects of the emperor, or men from warlike tribes outside the empire who were mercenaries (men who would fight for anyone who paid them). Some of the 'Roman' soldiers who fought in Britain were actually Germans.

As the western emperors grew too weak to control them, these armies began to fight each other. Then other fierce tribes, looking for loot, came to join in.

The most important of these last tribes were the Goths. By 493 the empire had come to an end, and Italy was a Gothic kingdom. But one important thing had survived from the Roman empire, and that was the Roman Catholic church. Its leader was the bishop of Rome, and people began to think of him as a successor to the emperors. The Roman church converted many of the Goths to Christianity. However, the next invaders were even fiercer. These were the Lombards, who invaded northern Italy and then tried to conquer Rome.

The bishop of Rome at that time was Gregory I (590–604). He was already a great religious leader, but now he had to be a commander as well. He fought off the Lombards with his own armies.

13

After that, the bishops of Rome (who came to be called Popes) had to be military rulers as well as bishops. They raised armies and fortified towns. As invasions and troubles went on, many Italians did the same. Walled cities grew up, especially in the north. In time they had their own governments, and controlled the land around them.

During the Middle Ages the city-states were very important. They had money, grand buildings, and rich trade; they produced great art. But they were rivals, and often at war. The greatest were Milan, Venice, Genoa, Pisa, and Florence.

In south Italy there was a different kind of state. Normans from northern France had conquered Sicily and the south by 1072. There they ruled people who took many of their ideas and customs from the Greeks and the Arabs.

So, by 1490, Italy was made up of many small states, all very different. In 1494 there was a French invasion in the north. After that, and for more than 300 years, France, Spain, and Austria fought for power over Italy. The state of Venice, with its sea-trading empire in the eastern Mediterranean, stayed free until 1797. The Popes kept their own states. Most of the rest was owned or controlled by foreign rulers until the 1840s. There were many revolts.

By 1848 there was a strong movement to free and unite Italy. The leader was the prime minister of one Italian kingdom, Piedmont-Sardinia. He was Camillo Benso di Cavour. Italy became an independent country, ruled by the king of Piedmont-Sardinia, in 1861. All but two of the states had joined by 1870. The Vatican City (the headquarters of the Roman Catholic Church) is a separate state ruled by the Pope. The City occupies about 44 hectares (108 acres) of the City of Rome. For the other state which remained independent, see San Marino.

The kingdom lasted until 1946, when Italy became a republic. Although it is now one united country there is still great variety among the people.

HOLLAND, also called THE NETHERLANDS

Before 1500 Holland had much the same history as Belgium, but with two big differences.

Holland was never part of the Roman empire. Tribes from north Germany, called Friesians, lived there. The Franks who were also from Germany, made Holland part of their empire after A.D. 800. The Franks and the Friesians had similar customs and spoke the same Germanic language. The people and language of Holland are called 'Dutch' in English.

Holland had a much longer coastline than Belgium. The Dutch had to spend a lot of time, thought, and money on building sea-walls to stop their flat land being flooded. Along the coast there were many small towns and villages; people had to live together in groups, to organize the work of protecting the coast.

The Dutch were good at trade. Their big trading cities were near the branches of the river Rhine which flowed out of Germany, through Holland, to the sea. Dutch merchants could travel by sea, or up the Rhine into the middle of Europe.

After 1500 there was a great reform of the Christian church in Europe. The Dutch took up new beliefs, which were called Protestant. They were especially impressed by the leading Protestant reformer and teacher, John Calvin.

The Hapsburg family were the overlords of Holland at that time: they ruled it from Spain.

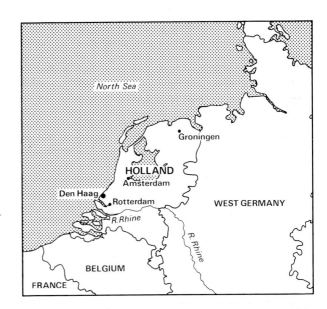

which was part of their empire. The Dutch resented having to pay taxes to a foreign overlord. When the Catholic Hapsburgs tried to stamp out their new religion, they rebelled. There was a war which ended in 1598. The Dutch won, and Holland became an independent country.

The new state was small and crowded, but the Dutch sent out fleets all over the world, finding profitable trade and founding colonies. They also began to make Holland bigger. They had always been good at keeping

In the sixteenth and seventeenth centuries the Dutch founded colonies in the East Indies. This painting shows a trading expedition returning to Amsterdam.

Along miles of coast, only the dykes hold back the sea. Here a dyke is breached during a storm in 1777.

15

the sea out; now they started to take land out of the sea. They built walls round land that was normally covered with water at high tide; they drained away the water that was there, and the walls prevented more water coming in. The land was very fertile.

Holland's inland frontiers have always been difficult to defend. The country has been invaded many times by the French and the Germans, up to the German invasion of 1940.

That occupation ended in 1945. Since then, the Dutch have been taking in new people from their old colonies; many of these were in the East and West Indies. Holland is still a crowded country, and the Dutch are still working to reclaim land from the sea.

Wool was an important industry in the Middle Ages. This ancient manuscript illustration shows a woman combing out the fibres of a fleece.

POLAND

Before A.D. 900 a tribe called the Polians used to live in the middle of Poland, around Poznan and Gniezno. They conquered the Masovian tribe who lived to the east, near what is now Warsaw.

The land which the Polians then ruled is the only place which has always been Polish. Even there, we have to say 'almost always', because there was a gap from 1793 to 1807.

Around this middle piece, the shape of Poland has been changing all the time.

The Polians went on to conquer the Silesians who lived south-west of them. They also took control of the country around Cracow in the south-east.

There was a narrow belt of land between Poland and Germany. There lived Slav tribes who were still pagan, like the Polians themselves. German warlords used to invade the Slav lands; the warlords often claimed to be good Catholics who were only fighting to

stamp out pagan beliefs. In 963 one of these warlords fought his way right across the belt of Slav land and attacked Poland.

The Polian chief at once made a pact with the German Emperor. The Emperor would stop any more attacks, and the Polians would be the Emperor's allies. The chief, Mieszko, also said that he would become a Christian and convert his people. That way, he got the Emperor's protection and took away the Germans' main excuse for attack.

Mieszko also made a pact with the Pope, who at that time was like a powerful prince. The Pope put the new, Catholic, Christian church in Poland under his own church of St Peter in Rome.

Mieszko had done all this as a sensible way of making Poland safe, but in time the Poles became genuine Catholics.

Now that they were allies and had the same religion, the Germans began to influence the Poles. The Poles learned a lot from the Germans, but they also began to worry in case the Germans were taking over. The pact did not last, and there were fights over land. Both countries wanted the Slav lands that lay between them and, most of all, the land to the north of Poland along the Baltic Sea.

The Poles' eastern neighbours were the states of early Russia. These states were often attacked by hordes of Mongols and Tartars from the east. In 1241 the hordes got through to the frontier of Poland, and the Poles had to fight them off. They won, but the war made them realize the dangers that could come from Russia. After that, they took some Russian land under their own control whenever they felt strong enough to do so.

Lithuania, which lay north-east of Poland, also won a huge area of Russian land. In 1386

the Queen of Poland was married to the Duke of Lithuania, Jagiello. The two countries formed a union with land all the way from the Baltic coast to the Black Sea. Poland became a very powerful country, and remained so until the Jagiello royal family died out in 1572.

By that time Poland's neighbours were very powerful too. There was a new, strong Russian state, ruled from Moscow. There was an Austrian empire to the south-west. Foreign princes were elected as kings of Poland; they dragged Poland into their own countries' quarrels.

In 1772 Austria, Russia, and Prussia (a new state in north Germany) all took parts of Poland. In 1793 Russia and Prussia took more. In 1795 all three countries took so much more that there was no Poland left. In 1809 the French emperor Napoleon drove them all out of central Poland, but he was defeated and his little Polish state came to an end.

In 1815 Poland became a country again, but much smaller, and with the Russian ruler as its king. For a hundred years the Russians tried to make the Poles Russian, with Russian language, education, and government. The other parts of the old Poland were either Prussian or Austrian; there, the language was German.

In 1918 Poland was recognized as an independent country, with new frontiers. For the first time since 1772 the Poles didn't need to use up all their energy trying to get rid of a foreign government. Now they could build new towns and ports, and set up industries in their country. But independence only lasted until 1939.

In 1939 Poland was invaded by Germany from the west and by Russia from the east, at the beginning of the Second World War. The war ended in 1945, and Poland's frontiers were changed again. Some German land was added to Poland in the west; Germans living there were turned out. Some Polish land was added to Russia in the east; Poles living there were turned out. At the same time, Russia took control of Poland's government.

Poland now has a western boundary roughly where it was in A.D. 1000. The eastern frontier is a new one, but its middle section is roughly the same as it was after the Russians had had their share in 1795.

NORWAY

Norway is a long, narrow country with a very long coast. The coast has hundreds of inlets, called fjords, cutting in to a mountain landscape. In the far north it is dark all the time during the winter. Most of the people of the north are Lapps, who live by herding reindeer.

For early Norwegians there was never enough good land. Local chieftains travelled with their people, looking for a place to settle. As Norway was mountainous it was easier to travel by boat up the coast, and settle in the sheltered fjords.

These people were of the type called Scandinavian. At first all Scandinavians (that is all the people of Denmark, Sweden, and Norway, except the Lapps) had the same language, customs, and religion. After about A.D. 800 they all sent out war-bands by sea, looking for plunder. Europeans called these raiders Vikings, whether they came from

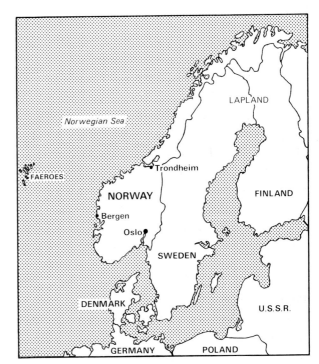

Norway, Sweden, or Denmark. Vikings were not always raiders and pirates; they founded colonies and started trade.

Norwegian Vikings settled in Iceland (in the north Atlantic) and the Faeroe Islands (north of the British Isles). Both these places became colonies of Norway. (The Arctic island of Spitsbergen did not become Norwegian until 1920.)

The Viking chiefs not only raided other countries, they attacked each other. Norway

Vikings from Scandinavia were great sea-raiders and settlers in the ninth and tenth centuries.

was not united under one king until 1015. This king was a Christian, St Olaf, and after his time Norway was slowly converted to Christianity. Norwegians also began to feel like a separate nation.

There were still civil wars, and it was usually the kings of Denmark who intervened when there was trouble. In 1537 Denmark took over Norway, Iceland, and the Faeroe Islands completely. The new Protestant form of Christianity came to Norway from Denmark, also.

The Danes held Norway until 1814. Then the Norwegians hoped for independence; instead they were joined with Sweden as two kingdoms under one (Swedish) king. They became more and more impatient with this, and in 1905 they gained independence with a king of their own.

Norwegians still depend on the sea; they have important merchant and fishing fleets. They also have cheap electricity from their fast mountain rivers; that makes life in the north a lot easier.

FRANCE

The people who lived in France in about 100 B.C. were called Gauls, a Celtic tribe. The Romans made France part of their empire. They conquered the south first, but it was about sixty years before they controlled all of it; the centre of France is mountainous, and the Gauls of the north were very fierce.

After A.D. 400 many tribes invaded the Roman empire. One of these, the Franks, won control of France. The Franks were Germans, but they were attracted by the life they found

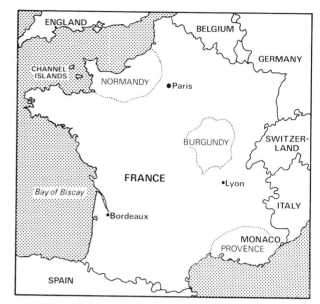

in France. The Gauls, who had become rather like Romans themselves, taught the Franks their language and their Roman ideas; they also took the Franks into their own Roman church.

The Frankish empire was divided in 843; after that, local rulers became more important. The empire had always used them, and their armies, to defend France. Now they were as powerful as the kings of France; the areas they ruled were like separate countries, and the most important were Normandy, Burgundy, and Provence.

Normandy was in the flat north. Normans were Vikings (sea-raiders from Norway and Denmark) who had settled there after 900. They were practical, and good organizers.

Burgundy was in the east, with big rivers that made travel and trade easy. Burgundians were energetic and full of new ideas.

Provence was in the south-east. The people had their own language, and many customs and ideas which had come from Italy or Greece. Provence had been one of the most

An incident during the Hundred Years War between France and England. Charles of Anjou is attacked by a British force at Fontenay.

'Roman' parts of France.

Other rulers held Brittany, in the far west, and Anjou, Aquitaine, and smaller states.

The king tried to keep his authority over all these places. His great ally was the Catholic church. Even after the kings had won absolute power, the church was still given the most important place in France, after the king.

After 1500 religion was reformed in Europe, and many people left the church to become Protestants. In France this was seen as a threat to the country itself, and there was civil war.

When the wars were over, the next three kings (who ruled from 1610 until 1774) were all determined to keep everybody under control.

In all the areas of France there were the same three groups of people. First, the clergy of the Catholic church; second, the noblemen (some of whom still held big areas of France); third, everybody else. All these groups had only the rights and the work which the king allowed them.

After 1700 the merchants, bankers, and manufacturers were discontented. They had founded colonies overseas, and built up trade.

They were rich enough to lend the king money. The country's economy depended on them. But the rules applied to their group stopped them from rising any higher in society, and from taking part in government. They were not even allowed to produce as much in business as they knew they could.

The noblemen were also discontented; the king had taken nearly all their real power away. All they had left was authority over the peasants on their own land. They began to enforce their local laws and taxes very severely.

The poor suffered; many had to leave their homes and beg.

In 1789 the noblemen rebelled against the king and ended most of his powers. But without the king they could not control the people. The businessmen saw their chance to get rid of all the old rules that held them back. When the noblemen tried to stop them they were killed. The poor joined in; crowds of

them caused all kinds of destruction. The rebellion became a revolution.

France became a republic in 1792. In 1799 one man, Napoleon Bonaparte, took control; he worked out a new code of law and an efficient government for the whole of France. He became the Emperor Napoleon.

There were two more periods of royal rule before France became a republic for good, which happened in 1870. By that time France was an industrial country. Most of the people were leaving the country to work in towns in the Paris area, or in the north-east. France today (and that includes Corsica) has about 54 million people, and those two areas are still the most crowded.

LUXEMBOURG

Luxembourg is a small country, bordered by Belgium, France, and Germany. It grew up round a fortress, which was the beginning of the city of Luxembourg. The fortress guarded a road, south of the Ardennes mountains, which was an important soldiers' route.

The early people were Celts, like the early French. Luxembourg was then part of the Roman empire until the fifth century; then it became part of the new empire of the Franks, a tribe from Germany. At that time 'Luxembourg' meant the present country and the southern part of what we call Belgium.

This area had a series of different overlords. An early Count of Luxembourg became emperor of Germany in 1308. The French Duke of Burgundy ruled Luxembourg from

Louis Napoleon, President of the Republic, became the last Emperor of France in 1852–70.

1443, and later it passed to the Hapsburg family whose empire spread from Austria.

During the nineteenth century Luxembourg was linked with Holland. The country got its present shape in 1839, when part of it passed to Belgium; it became an independent country in 1867.

With such a history, the people naturally speak French and German as well as their own language, Letzeburgesch (or Luxemburgisch). Like their Belgian neighbours, they are Roman Catholic in religion.

YUGOSLAVIA

The land which is now Yugoslavia used to have two tribes. The Illyrians lived in the west and the Thracians in the east. They were there in A.D. 9 when the Romans made the whole area into a province of their empire. The Romans called it Illyricum.

In 395 the Romans divided their empire in two. The dividing line ran down through Yugoslavia. The north and west were still ruled from Rome; ideas, customs, and language were the same as those of other Roman-ruled places in western Europe. The south and east were ruled from Istanbul, which was then called Constantinople (ancient Byzantium); that was the capital of the eastern or Greek-speaking empire.

In these two empires two kinds of Christian church developed: the Roman Catholic in the west and the Greek Orthodox in the east.

The empires were often invaded. During the sixth century a new race arrived from eastern Europe. These were the Slavs. In time they took over most of the country and set up seven Slav states.

Slovenia was in the north-west. The Slovene Slavs became Roman Catholics. Their history became linked to that of the powerful Catholic countries next door – the German empire and, later, the Austrian empire. The country became part German-speaking, part Slovene.

Croatia was in the north. The Croatian Slavs, or Croats, were also converted to the Roman Catholic faith. They learned to write their language in the Roman alphabet. They had many years of rule by the Catholic state of Hungary.

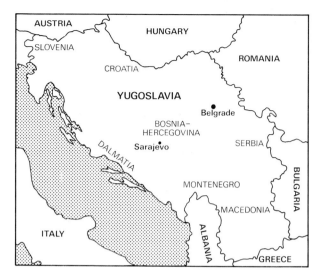

Serbia was in the east. The Serbs, or Serbian Slavs, spoke a version of the Croats' language, which is still called Serbo-Croat. But they used an eastern alphabet like the one used today in Russia. They learned this from missionaries of the Orthodox church who converted them; it was called the Cyrillic alphabet after the missionary St Cyril. Serbia was an important country; by 1355 Serbian land stretched down into Greece and Albania.

Bosnia-Hercegovina was in the middle. The people never came wholly under eastern or western influence. Many followed the Bogomil religion which was not Christian, although it included some Christian ideas.

Dalmatia was the coastal strip of land, where people lived by shipping, sea-trade, and piracy. Hungary, Austria, and the Italian city of Venice all wanted to rule this coast, and Dalmatia was caught in their quarrels.

Macedonia, in the south-east, had many shapes and many overlords. The state developed as a mixture of Slavs, Bulgarians,

A Slav army in Hercegovina in 1875 plans an attack on an advancing Turkish column.

24

Albanians, and Greeks.

Montenegro lay south of Dalmatia, in the mountains. The country was so wild and the people so fierce that no one was able to conquer it. Montenegro was founded in 1356 and remained independent through all its history until 1945.

All the other states were caught in the great wars between the countries of central Europe and the invading Turks. The Turks were Moslems from Asia, who wanted to conquer the whole of the eastern empire. They made their first attacks on Yugoslavia in the fourteenth century. The armies of Austria and Hungary came to drive them out. When the wars ended, Turkey controlled Macedonia, Serbia, and Bosnia-Hercegovina; Austria or Hungary controlled Slovenia, Croatia, and Dalmatia.

Turkish rule ended in Bosnia-Hercegovina in 1908. Austria took control instead. Many Bogomils had become Moslems under the Turks, and they now rebelled against Catholic Austria. Serbia also encouraged risings. Serbia had kept her Orthodox faith and Slav identity under Turkish rule. She had now become an independent kingdom, urging other Slavs to work for freedom. The Turks had been driven from all states by 1913; Austro-Hungarian rule ended in 1918.

A new country was then formed, called the Kingdom of the Serbs, Croats, and Slovenes; it was ruled by the king of Serbia. In 1945 the kingdom became a republic with the name of Yugoslavia, which means 'South Slav'. There are six states: Serbia, Croatia (including Dalmatia), Bosnia-Hercegovina, Slovenia, Montenegro, and Macedonia.

ANDORRA

Andorra is a republic lying on the border between France and Spain in the Pyrenees mountains. The people are of French and Spanish descent, and both languages are spoken; the official language is Catalan, a kind of Spanish. The President of France and the Bishop of Urgel (in Spain) jointly rule Andorra. (See map of Spain)

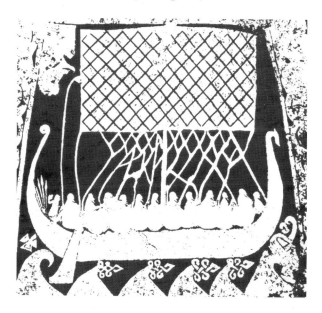

A huge slab of stone, decorated in medieval times with a carving of a Viking ship.

SWEDEN

The earliest important kingdom that we know about was in the region where Stockholm is now. This was the kingdom of the Svear people. The other important areas were not on the mainland of Sweden but the Baltic Sea islands of Gotland and Öland.

The Romans wrote about the Svear people before A.D. 400; they said they had a good fleet, were good at trade, and loved riches.

After about 800 a new people from Sweden became widely known. These were the Vikings – a name for all the sea-pirates who sailed out raiding from the Baltic Sea, and from the North Sea coasts of Norway and Denmark as well. Vikings from Sweden went eastwards up the Baltic, along the coast of Finland, and into the mouths of Russian rivers. They sailed far into Russia and found the great trade routes into eastern Asia. They became merchants as well as pirates; once again, Sweden became rich through trade.

However, the country was still quite small. What is now the southern tip of Sweden was then part of Denmark, and the north had

hardly been explored. Olof Skötkonung was king of Sweden from about the year 1000; he ruled only Öland and Gotland, the old Svear lands around Stockholm, and two areas to the west of it called Ostergotland and Vastergotland.

Olof was the first Christian king, but the Swedes still believed in the Vikings' gods; they were not converted in large numbers until after 1100.

During the fourteenth century Sweden conquered Finland; she then enlarged her own territory by clearing the forests of the north. Small farmers settled there to work the land. German miners settled in the mountains to mine iron and copper. German merchants set up small towns where they bought the metal for export.

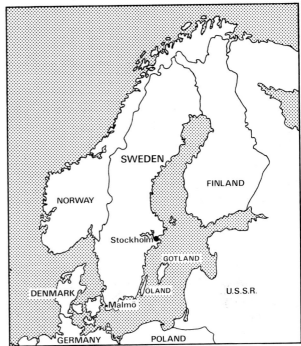

It was through Germans that the Protestant religion came to Sweden in the sixteenth century. The new beliefs, taught by the German reformer Martin Luther, were established in Sweden by 1550.

When the German Protestant states were attacked by the German Emperor, the Swedish king Gustavus Adolphus (1611–32) led his armies into Germany to defend them.

The Battle of Lutzen in 1632 was a brilliant victory for the Swedes in the Thirty Years War. Their leader, Gustavus Adolphus, was one of the great military geniuses of history.

Sweden became very important during these religious wars, as well as becoming the friend of many German states.

There were wars with Denmark. Both countries wanted to be the strongest in the area around the Baltic Sea. In 1660 the Swedes conquered the Danish land in south Sweden, which was very fertile.

During the next hundred years Russia became more important in north Europe and Sweden less so. Russia drove the Swedes out of Finland in 1808. In 1814 Sweden began a union with Norway which lasted until 1905.

Since then Sweden has had its present shape. The north reaches up into the Arctic, where the winters are dark and bitterly cold; most of the people live in the south. Like their neighbours in Norway and Denmark, they are of the type called Scandinavian.

BULGARIA

Bulgaria has two big rivers. The Danube flows through low-lying country in the north, the Maritsa through its own valley further south. In between the two, and in the far south, there are mountains.

The Thracians, famous as horsemen, were the early people of Bulgaria; they were conquered by the Macedonians under King Philip II (359–336 B.C.). Many Macedonians were of Thracian descent, and the two peoples mingled easily. However, Macedonia's empire was conquered by the Romans, and in 46 B.C. Bulgaria became part of the Roman empire.

In A.D. 395 the empire was divided in two. Bulgaria was part of the eastern half. The eastern emperor ruled from a Greek-speaking

In the Eastern Christian Church, an icon is a sacred picture of an angel or saint. This one in a thirteenth-century church depicts St George the Crowned.

28

city, Byzantium (which is now Istanbul). Greek was the language of the eastern empire; when Christianity spread, it did so in the form of the Greek Orthodox church.

The emperors were seldom strong enough to keep out enemies. Bulgaria was on the edge of the empire, and it was invaded by two powerful tribes. The Slavs came from eastern Europe in the sixth century. Slav language and ways of life spread through the country. Then in the seventh century the Bulgars came. They did not swamp the Slavs as the Slavs had swamped the original people. Instead, they learned the Slavs' language and copied their customs. Both tribes in time became Orthodox Christians.

The Bulgars fitted in to the eastern empire quite well, but their leaders would not always agree to be ruled by the emperor. Sometimes they broke away altogether. During the ninth and tenth centuries they conquered more land and set up an empire of their own; the emperor brought them back under his control in 1018.

The Turks, who were Moslems, invaded the empire from Asia. They defeated the Bulgars in 1371 and had control of Bulgaria before 1400.

The Turks allowed the Bulgarian language and the Orthodox church to survive. But during the nineteenth century Turkish rule

The Valley of Roses, where millions of rose bushes are grown for the manufacture of Attar of Roses.

became very harsh. Bulgarians wanted to be free. They got their freedom in 1908, but they also wanted the new, free country to be much bigger. There had been links between Bulgaria and Macedonia since before Roman times; now there were many Bulgarians living in Macedonia; they wanted their country to be part of the new Bulgaria.

There were wars, and many arguments about the frontiers. Bulgaria's present frontiers were not fixed until 1947.

During the Second World War Bulgaria took Germany's side against Russia. Russia invaded Bulgaria in 1944, and set up a government that was friendly to Russia. The present communist People's Republic was founded in 1946.

GERMANY

There used to be many tribes in Germany. All had different customs, but their languages were alike. They were the Germanic languages, and the tribes came to be called Germanic, or German. The most important were the Franks, Saxons, Bavarians, Alemanni, Thuringians, and Friesians. Until about A.D. 400 their western boundary was the River Rhine.

By A.D. 804 the Franks had conquered all the others. They had also conquered France, and Charlemagne the Frank ruled France and Germany. His grandsons divided his empire in 843. Germany was then separated from France; for centuries there were arguments about where the dividing line should be.

Germany had hundreds of states, some big and important, some tiny. Apart from the

mountains of the south there were few natural defences. In 911 the last Frankish king died, and the small states knew they could not fight off their enemies on their own. They chose a new king as a warlord to protect them against Danes in the north, and Slavs and Magyars in the east. The states had to help the king with the actual fighting; for many years it was normal for a German state to be run like an army.

In 962 the king, Otto I, was made an emperor. He was crowned in Rome, by the Pope, as Holy Roman Emperor. He was supposed to be the Roman Catholic leader of what had once been the Roman Empire in Europe. From then on, German kings became more and more involved with things outside Germany. The state rulers took more power for themselves. They became rivals for power and there were frequent wars.

After 1100 many states had more people than they could feed. They cut down the forests and drained the marshes to make farmland. They also moved eastwards on to land that belonged to the Slavs. They had beaten the Slavs in battles before, but this time German soldiers were followed by thousands of German settlers. The land was good for grain, and became important in trade.

The rulers of smaller states tried to keep out of the wars. They competed in peaceful things, like commerce and learning. German merchants formed a powerful league, called the Hanseatic League, to build up their trade. The League became strong enough to set up German colonies in many trading cities of north Europe. State rulers set up universities, and encouraged printing. Then educated men all over Germany were able to read and discuss each others' work. People were

Opposite: Before the majestic Brandenburg Gate lies the modern wall, built by the East Germans in 1961 to separate the two halves of Berlin.

Before the Worms parliament in 1521, Luther refused to revoke his teachings against Catholic doctrine.

reminded that they had a language in common; whichever state they lived in, they were all Germans and they did form a nation.

One of the new German scholars was Martin Luther. In 1517 he set out to reform the Catholic church. Many German Christians followed him. A new German church broke away from Catholicism and called itself Lutheran. Whole states took up the new faith.

The Emperor, as a Catholic ruler, tried to win them back by force. There were wars until 1648. By then Austria and the rest of south Germany were still Catholic. North Germany was Lutheran, and its most important state was Prussia, in the north-east.

Prussia lay on the grain lands which had been taken from the Slavs. A Prussian's main work was to farm the land and support the army. Prussia became more powerful until, in

1871, she was able to set up a new united Germany; Prussia's main rival, Austria, was not included.

This time, national unity was a fact and not just a feeling. But many states resented Prussian control. After the First World War the Prussian king of Germany had to abdicate, and there was a republic instead, founded in 1919.

The frontiers were changed by the two world wars (1914–18 and 1939–45). The main arguments were about the frontiers with France, with Poland, and with Czechoslovakia.

The united Germany came to an end in 1945, and now there are two German states. The Federal Republic in the west includes many of the old small states (now called Lands); it still has a Catholic south and a mainly Lutheran north. The Democratic Republic is a communist state; it was formed in the Russian occupation after 1945, in what used to be Prussia.

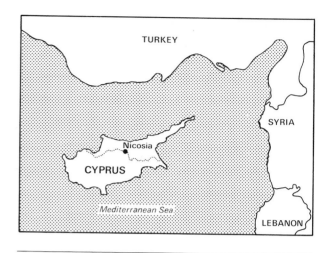

CYPRUS

The republic of Cyprus is a small island in the eastern Mediterranean Sea. Its nearest neighbours are Turkey and Syria (both in Asia).

The earliest invaders that we know about were Greek. They came as traders in about 1400 B.C. Later, more Greeks came and settled there. Greek life and the Greek language spread through the island.

By A.D. 60 Cyprus was part of the Roman empire. At about that time St Paul and St Barnabas visited Cyprus and converted the Roman ruler to Christianity. The Roman empire split in two in A.D. 395. Cyprus was part of the eastern, Greek-speaking, half; Christianity in Cyprus took the form which was called Greek Orthodox.

The empire came to an end gradually, as the emperors failed to keep their enemies out. During the twelfth century armies from

Charlemagne, King of the Franks, was crowned as the first Holy Roman Emperor by the Pope on Christmas Day, A.D. 800, in St Peter's Church in Rome.

The Roman mosaic on the right shows an incident in Cypriot life. Cyprus became a Roman province in 58 B.C.

western Europe invaded the area. Cyprus was held by western European rulers until 1571, when it was taken by Turkey. The Turks held it until 1914.

During all that time the original Greek people survived. The western invaders had little effect on their life, customs, and language. The Turks, however, had come from only a few miles away; they found it easy to settle in north Cyprus in large numbers. By 1914 there were two communities; the Greeks were, and still are, the larger of the two.

Cyprus was British from 1914 until 1959. Since then there have been various outbreaks of fighting. Many Greeks would like Cyprus to be part of Greece, and many Turks would like it to be part of Turkey. In 1983 the leader of the Turks declared the Turkish part of the island to be an independent state. Arguments about how to settle the problem continue.

FAEROES

The Faeroes is a group of a very small islands which lies to the north of the British Isles. Viking sailors from Norway landed there about A.D. 800. At that time the only inhabitants were monks, whom the Vikings drove out. The islands were then ruled by Norway until 1537, when they became Danish.

ROMANIA

Romania is the most easterly country on the river Danube. The river flows through the south to a big delta on the Black Sea coast. Northern Romania is mountainous.

The early people were Thracians, living as herdsmen, and moving into defended villages when there was danger. The Romans conquered them and called their land Dacia. The people accepted Roman rule and customs. The Romanian language has much in common with the Romans' language, Latin.

After A.D. 270 the Romans had to leave Dacia undefended, as their empire had grown too big to protect. People moved away from the Danube plain, which was easy to invade; they went to the mountains of Transylvania, and there lived safe from invasion for centuries.

In 896 the Magyars, a warlike people from the east, conquered Transylvania. Not only the Magyars but, later, the Germans (who were the Magyars' allies) came to live in it. Romanians living in Transylvania had to put up with two sorts of foreigners, two foreign languages, and a western religion – the

Roman Catholic church. Many left the mountains and moved back to the lowlands.

In the early fourteenth century the Romanians founded two independent states. Wallachia was in the south and Moldavia was in the east. There they had their own kind of Christianity, the Eastern Orthodox church which had spread through the eastern part of the old Roman empire, to which Romania had belonged.

This old empire was now being attacked by Turks, Moslems from Asia. Wallachia came under Turkish control in 1393, Moldavia in 1455. By that time Transylvania was not only ruled by Magyars but was joined to the Magyar kingdom of Hungary. The Turks conquered it in 1526 and the people (Romanians, Magyars, and Germans) came under Turkish rule.

The Turks did not force people to become Moslems. Many did, but the Orthodox church survived in Wallachia and Moldavia, and so did the Catholic church in Transylvania. After 1526 Transylvania also had two of the new Protestant Christian sects: many Germans

On the opposite page, a priest tries to persuade Romanian peasants to go peacefully away, during an uprising at Braila in 1907.

became followers of Martin Luther, and many Magyars became followers of John Calvin. In 1699 Transylvania was recaptured by the new rulers of Hungary, who were Catholics, but by that time the Protestant churches were firmly set up.

Moldavia and Wallachia were part of the Turkish empire until 1878. Then they became independent, and joined together as the state of Romania (in those days it was usually spelt Rumania).

In 1918–19 Transylvania broke away from Hungary and joined Romania; however, it still has many Germans and Magyars living there. Also in 1919 Romania gained some land to the east; this was lost again (to Russia) at the end of the Second World War in 1945. Romania was very important during that war, because she had large oil-fields which countries on both sides wanted.

Modern Romania is a republic, with a communist government.

CZECHOSLOVAKIA

There are three parts to Czechoslovakia: Bohemia (the western part), Moravia (the middle part), and Slovakia (the eastern part).

In Bohemia and Moravia the early tribes were driven out by Germanic people. The country lay along the edge of the Roman empire. Germanic tribes came together all along this edge; while the empire lasted, it was as far as they could get. They settled in Bohemia and Moravia, but before A.D. 500 they had been invaded in their turn, by Slavs. The Slavs came from what is now Russia; they moved west through Europe as far as the mountains of Austria and the big rivers of eastern Germany. Different Slav tribes invaded all three parts of Czechoslovakia. Those who came to Bohemia and Moravia were Czechs; those who came to Slovakia were Slovaks. They still speak separate (but similar) languages.

During the ninth century Moravia became the centre of an empire called Great Moravia. This included Bohemia, Slovakia, present-day Hungary, and parts of what are now Germany and Poland.

The people were converted to Christianity. For a long time it was not certain whether they would turn to the Roman Catholic church or the Eastern Orthodox church. Most Slav countries became Orthodox. However, Roman Catholic missionaries from the German state of Bavaria, next door, made the Czechs Roman Catholic. At about the same time, Slovakia was conquered by the Magyars. These people came from the east but they were not Slavs. Their kingdom was Hungary; Slovakia was part of Hungary until 1918.

The empire of Great Moravia came to an end. In 1029 Moravia and Bohemia became a new country under one prince. The country was independent, but the prince had an overlord, the German emperor. Bohemia also had many German settlers, especially near the western frontier; they helped with farming the land, mining metals, and building towns.

When the native rulers died out in 1306, it seemed natural to offer the throne to a German prince.

The second German prince to rule the Czechs became German emperor as well. He made the country part of a league of Catholic states. The Catholic church became very rich. The Czechs thought of it as a German church. They resented its wealth, and they wanted a Czech church where they could worship in their own language.

A Czech priest, Jan Huss, began to reform the church after 1390; he also encouraged the use of the Czech language in church. His followers turned his campaign into a national revolt. Armies of 'Hussites' fought the armies

Prague, the capital city, has many fine old buildings and statues. Here crowds gather in front of the astronomical clock on the wall of the Town Hall.

of the emperor.

However, the Hussites could not agree with each other. Hussite landowners were jealous of rich Hussite towns, and frightened of the peasant armies, so the Czechs could not unite.

In 1526 another German ruler became king of Bohemia and Moravia. He was Ferdinand of Hapsburg, Duke of Austria. Under Hapsburg rule there were more revolts; all failed, with a final defeat in 1620. After that, the Hapsburgs made sure that the country remained Catholic and German-speaking.

The Hapsburgs built up an enormous empire of German, Magyar, and Slav peoples. The Czechs lived as part of this empire until 1918. They were well ruled by the Hapsburgs on the whole, but many disliked being turned into Austrians. As the Hapsburgs were rulers of Austria and ran their huge empire from Austria, this is what was happening.

By 1800 all the more important people spoke German; the peasants and the poorer townspeople spoke Czech. However, the Czech-speakers became better off and better educated, through social reforms. They turned to their fellow-Slavs in nearby countries for support. Then they began to work for freedom from Austria.

The Austrian empire broke up in 1918. An independent Czechoslovakia was founded; it included Slovakia as well as Bohemia and Moravia.

In 1938 the Germans took the parts of Bohemia which had a mainly German population. In 1939 they conquered the rest of the country. The German invaders were driven out in 1945; by that time the Czechs were feeling strongly anti-German, and they drove out many of their own German-speaking people too.

A communist government then took power, and Czechoslovakia joined the Slav group of communist countries in eastern Europe.

GREECE

The mainland of Greece is mountainous, with the Pindus range running down the middle. Greece also includes many islands in the Aegean Sea, and some – the Ionian Islands – in the Adriatic. Modern Greece stretches north and east across fertile farmland; early Greece was much smaller.

The biggest island is Crete. Here, an earlier people than the Greeks were already rich and civilized before 2000 B.C. Crete was a stopping place for seafarers between Europe, Africa, and the Middle East. But the Aegean was a place of earthquakes and volcanoes. The kingdom of Crete ended suddenly; it was probably destroyed when the nearby volcano of Santorini blew up.

The first Greeks came from north of the Aegean, and settled all round its shores. They arrived in mainland Greece about 2000 B.C. There were two important tribes already there: the people of Attica, whose centre was Athens, and the people of Arcadia, whose centre was Argos.

The early Greeks became very powerful. Mycenae was the main fortress of great warlords for about 700 years. Then there was another invasion. The Dorians, who also came from the north, spoke a kind of Greek. They were less civilized than the Greeks but just as warlike. Southern Greeks began to come together in fortified cities, for defence. In time these cities became the centres of states. The most important were Athens, Sparta, Argos, Corinth, and Thebes.

The people of the states produced great art, ideas, and forms of government which have influenced a large part of the world ever since.

They founded colonies all round the Aegean coast (much of modern Turkey was Greek at that time). But they were often at war with each other as they competed for sea-power.

North of the Greek states lay Macedonia and Thessaly; there lived Thracians and Illyrians (from what are now Bulgaria and Yugoslavia) as well as Greeks. Macedonia – under Philip II and Alexander – conquered Thessaly and Greece and made one, big, Greek empire. This empire was conquered by the Romans in 148 B.C.

The Romans admired the Greeks; they copied their art and studied their ideas. When the Roman empire was divided in A.D. 395, the emperor of the eastern part set up his capital at Byzantium. This city (later called Constantinople, and now Istanbul) had been a Greek colony; it became a centre of Greek culture which spread through the eastern empire. In time, eastern Christians broke away from the Christian church of Rome and founded the Greek Orthodox church.

This eastern empire and its Greek culture lasted until the fifteenth century, but it was not always strong enough to keep out invaders. Slavs from eastern Europe settled in Greece after the year 500, learned the Greek language, and became Orthodox Christians. Later on, there were Albanian settlers and Vlachs from Romania.

Armies from western Europe also attacked the empire, looking for plunder. The Greeks disliked and distrusted the west, especially the Italian states. They sometimes felt they had more in common with their eastern neighbours, the Turks. When the Turks invaded the

Salonika, with its many mosques, was still a Turkish city when this picture was drawn in 1876.

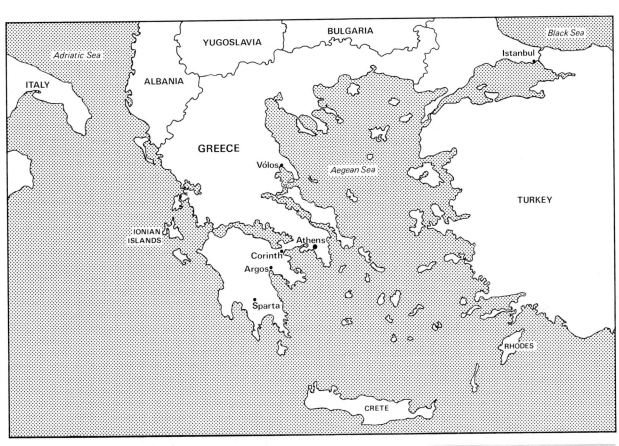

eastern empire from Asia, they were able to win the whole of Greece by 1460.

The Turks gave most of their attention to the fertile land and the cities. They left the mountain people alone. They also tolerated the Greek language and the Orthodox Christian faith. Only in the last years of Turkish rule was there cruel oppression. The Greeks rebelled in 1821, and began to drive the Turks out. By 1832 there was a new, independent Greece.

The new state was small. It included the mainland as far north as the Gulf of Volos, and some of the islands in the Aegean. There was not much fertile land, which was still held by Turkey.

The Greeks remembered that they had once had a great empire. They objected to the new frontiers. During the next hundred years they slowly added to their land, until they got their present country which is more than twice as big as that of 1832. Macedonia is now divided; the name is used for a part of northern Greece and for a part of southern Yugoslavia.

Left, a tiny town on the Aegean island of Siphnos. Right, the amphitheatre at Dodona, famed since classical times as the site of the oldest Greek oracle.

SWITZERLAND

The west and centre of Switzerland are made up of high, hilly country which is good for farming and growing vines. Most of the rest is mountains, with deep river valleys in between.

The Romans invaded Switzerland after 58 B.C. The people they conquered were Celts. The river Rhine, which was the Romans' northern frontier, still forms most of the northern boundary of Switzerland.

When the Romans left, tribes from Germany began coming across the Rhine to settle in north and central Switzerland. Other tribes of Burgundians (from part of what is now France) settled in the west. Italian tribes moved into the south. Only in the east were the 'Romanized' Celts left in control.

There are still four groups of Swiss, speaking German, French, Italian, and an old Roman-Celtic language called Romansch.

In the Middle Ages much of Switzerland belonged to a few powerful families. The most powerful were the Hapsburgs. They became rulers of Austria and emperors of all the German states.

Most people in Switzerland lived in communes. These were small groups of people who kept together so as to make the best of their farmland, pasture, woods, and fresh water. When the Hapsburgs became very powerful, the communes began to join together to defend their rights, and to form leagues.

These leagues were the beginning of the present Swiss states, or cantons. They fought for independence from the German emperor, and fought off outside enemies from Italy and Savoy (an old state which became part of Italy and, later, part of France). They also fell out with each other. There was a lot of warfare. By the time they had won independence in 1499, Swiss soldiers were probably the best in Europe. Swiss men often earned a living by fighting in the armies of other countries.

During the sixteenth century the Christian church in Europe was reformed. Switzerland was (and still is) divided between the old Catholic and the new Protestant beliefs.

All the present states came together in a union in 1848.

Outside the big towns people still live in communes. Each commune has some good land, some pasture, some woodland, and enough water. The group of people is kept together in the river valley; the communes are separated from each other by the mountains. So Switzerland is a gathering of many small units, all of which like to be as independent as possible.

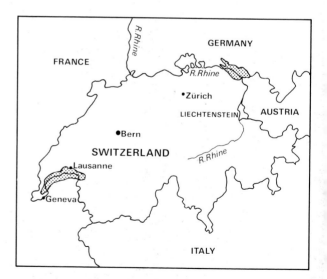

The Swiss have been exporters of cheese for centuries. Here a peasant of the Toggenburg district makes the cheese in a large copper kettle over an open fire.

UNITED KINGDOM

The name 'United Kingdom' means the United Kingdom of Great Britain and Northern Ireland. Great Britain is the great or large island of the British Isles; it is made up of England, Scotland, and Wales.

The Romans visited England in 55 B.C.; they found Celtic tribes very like the people they had conquered in France. Celts were lively and clever. They were also warlike; much of their skill in metalwork was used to make weapons and armour.

The Romans invaded England in A.D. 43; conquest took forty years. Then the tribes of England became used to Roman ways of living and Roman law. They took up the Christian religion as it spread through the Roman empire.

The religion also reached Wales, but the Welsh Celts were not much affected by Roman rule in other ways. Their country was mountainous and difficult to conquer.

The same was true of the Scottish Celts, although for a short time the Romans had a northern frontier in central Scotland. All the tribes who lived beyond it were known to the Romans as Picts (painted ones) because they decorated themselves with patterns like tattoos. After A.D. 196 the frontier moved south to Hadrian's Wall, which runs between the Solway Firth and the mouth of the river Tyne.

Then the Scottish tribes were independent again, although some were allies of the Romans against the Picts. Other Celts came from Ireland to settle in Scotland, mainly in the south and west.

Roman rule in England ended after A.D.

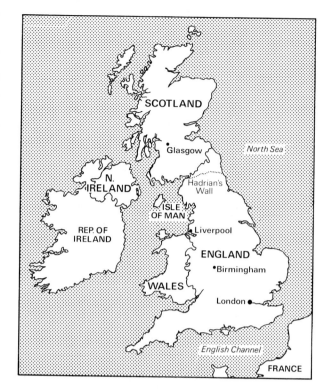

400. The English Celts had no unity. After 450 there were more invaders, and the Celts could not band together to keep them out. These new people were from north-west Germany and parts of Denmark. They were Angles, who settled in eastern England and Scotland, Jutes who settled in Kent, and Saxons who came to the south and spread northwards.

None of these had ever been Roman subjects. Wherever they settled and took control, Roman life died out. We do not know what happened to the Christian religion in England; the Celts probably kept their beliefs but lost their organized church. Christianity was brought in again in 597.

In time the invaders came to control most of

The last successful invasion was in 1066. After the Battle of Hastings, William of Normandy proclaimed himself king of England.

Oſquodum vero idem·

Guillermus dux·m die natalis domini ab Aelando

England, although Cornwall and Cumbria remained Celtic for a long time.

After 800 pirates from Denmark and Norway, called Vikings, began to raid the coasts of the British Isles. Then they began to settle in places they had raided. Viking villages grew up around the coasts of Ireland and Scotland and in south-west Wales and the Isle of Man. It was mainly Vikings from Denmark who came to England. They conquered the north and east. In 1013 England had a Danish king and was for a time part of the Danish empire.

By 1065, before the last invasion, the people of Great Britain were already mixed. England had Celts, Saxons, Angles, Jutes, and Vikings. Wales had Celts and some Viking settlements. Scotland had Picts, other Celts, Angles, and Vikings.

The last invaders were Normans. These men came from northern France; their ancestors had been Vikings who had settled there. Their duke, William, conquered England in 1066.

Normans spoke a kind of French, and this became the language of all educated and important people (except in the church, which used Latin). As the English language developed it included many French words. The Norman kings gave England a link with France that lasted for about 400 years.

Scotland had a link with France, too, especially south-eastern Scotland. There were also strong links with Norman England. The language spoken in southern Scotland was a mixture of northern English, Norse (the

By the early nineteenth century England was the world's centre of trade and commerce. Here is a view of the great wool floor at London docks.

Viking language), and Norman French. The Celts still lived in their tribes or clans in the west and north; they spoke Gaelic, a Celtic language.

Welsh is also a Celtic language. The kings of England conquered Wales in 1282, but at first this did not have much effect on the language. They did bring in English law instead of Welsh Celtic law. During the sixteenth century they also began to make Wales more English; they brought in the English language, and the English church.

It was also at that time that the new Protestant religion came to Great Britain. During the next hundred years there were civil wars; arguments about religion were tangled up with arguments about national freedom, or different kinds of government.

In 1603 the king of Scotland, James VI, became James I of England as well. However, the two countries did not have one shared government until 1707. Ireland had been partly ruled by the kings of England since the twelfth century; they had control of all of it by 1600, and Ireland did not become independent until 1921. Then the north-east corner chose to remain under English rule.

After 1760 there were two big changes that produced further mixing of nationalities. There were new industries; people moved round the country looking for work in the new factory towns. There was new interest in countries overseas; people from all parts of the British Isles founded colonies abroad. The colonies became an empire and, later, a Commonwealth.

In the twentieth century this Commonwealth sent many people to live in Britain; most of them came from India, Pakistan, and the West Indies.

*Two knights of the order of St John of Jerusalem. In
1530 Malta became their headquarters.*

48

MALTA

Malta is a group of five islands which lie south of Sicily in the Mediterranean sea. The biggest island (also called Malta), Gozo, and Comino, are inhabited. Comminotto and Filfla are not; they are very tiny.

People have lived in Malta since at least 3800 B.C. The Carthaginians from north Africa were there from about 600 B.C.; they lost Malta to the Romans in 218 B.C.

As a part of the Roman empire, Malta became Christian; the people are thought to have been converted by St Paul.

After A.D. 395 Malta was supposed to be part of the eastern half of the Roman empire. In fact the Arabs, from north Africa and the Middle East, had more effect on life and ideas than the eastern empire did. After the year 1000 there was frequent contact with Sicily. The Maltese language developed as a mixture of Sicilian and Arabic.

During the Middle Ages European knights formed a company, or Order, to protect Christian pilgrims visiting Jerusalem. They were called the Order of the Hospital of St John of Jerusalem. In 1530 Malta became their main base in the Mediterranean; Valetta, the capital, was their fortress. It was named after their Grand Master, Jean de la Valette. Malta was attacked more than once by the knights' enemies; Maltese outside Valetta tended to live in groups of villages, easily defended.

In 1798 Malta was conquered by the French. In 1802 it was given back to the knights. The Maltese protested at this. The knights left, and Malta became a British colony in 1814.

Malta was still an ideal base for a navy in the Mediterranean. It became a military base for the British as it had been for the knights. By the end of the Second World War, in 1945, the Maltese had had enough. They wanted to control their own future, and be something other than a fortress. Malta became an independent country in 1964. The British base closed in 1979.

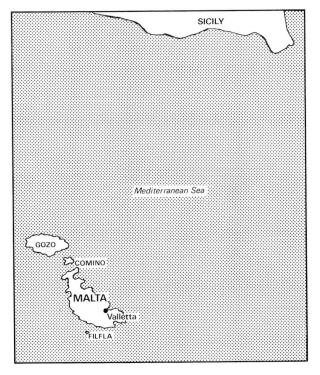

MONACO

Monaco is a very small state, set into the Mediterranean coast of France, near Nice. The people speak French and Monégasque, which is a mixture of French and Italian. Since 1297 they have been ruled by the Grimaldi family, Princes of Monaco. (See map of France.)

DENMARK

Denmark is a flat country almost surrounded by sea. There is a peninsula and a group of islands. No place in Denmark is far from the North Sea or the Baltic Sea.

The people are Scandinavians, like their neighbours the Norwegians and the Swedes. All Scandinavian people began with the same language, and the same customs, and worshipped the same gods: Woden, Thor, and Freyr. They admired a good fighter and were impressed by wealth.

After about A.D. 750 some of these people became pirates and sea-raiders; these were known as Vikings. Danish Vikings raided England, France, and North Germany, and were greatly feared.

After A.D. 900 there was a slow change. The Danes were becoming Christian, and were also forming themselves into a separate country, with a king. Even the Vikings turned to trade instead of looting. Many left Denmark and settled down in the lands they had raided.

The Danes who stayed were mainly farmers, fishermen, and sailors. Denmark had a navy and an important merchant fleet. Much of Danish history is about Danes, Swedes, and North Germans competing for control of the Baltic Sea. At first the Danes held south Sweden and controlled both sides of the entrance to the Baltic. In 1537 they took over Norway and the far-away Norwegian settlements in the Faeroe Islands and Iceland.

In 1660 the Swedes drove the Danes out of south Sweden, so the Danes lost their best farmland and their hold on the Baltic Sea. They still had trade in the north Atlantic, with Iceland and the Faeroe Islands; in 1721 they

The area of Schleswig-Holstein was disputed between Denmark and Germany for centuries. Here, Danish artillery and infantry are in action in 1850.

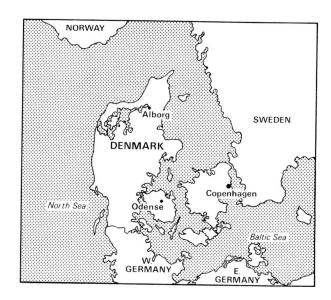

50

went even further north-west and founded a colony in Greenland in north America. In 1814 they had to give up Norway, but they kept the Faeroes and Iceland.

Denmark has one land frontier. This is the German frontier of south Denmark. German families have moved into Denmark from earliest times, and so have German ideas. Denmark was one of the first countries to adopt the teaching of Martin Luther (the German religious reformer) in the sixteenth century. But there have been wars, too. The southern frontier has been moved more than once. On either side of it there are still areas of mixed population: people of Danish descent living in what is now Germany, and *vice versa*.

Denmark is still a kingdom. Greenland and the Faeroe Islands are still part of the kingdom, but Iceland is an independent country.

ISLE OF MAN

The Isle of Man is a part of the British Isles and is situated in the Irish Sea. It belongs to the British Crown. The people are called Manx; they are of Celtic and Viking descent. (See map of United Kingdom)

CHANNEL ISLANDS

The Channel Islands (Jersey, Guernsey, Alderney, Sark, and others) are in the English Channel and belong to the British Crown. The people are of French and English descent. (See map of France)

Jersey, in the Channel Islands, was the site of the last French invasion against Britain. This famous painting depicts an episode in the Battle of Jersey in 1781.

HUNGARY

The size of Hungary has changed many times. It has been a very small place in the west of the present country; it has also been big enough to embrace the eastern part of Czechoslovakia, the western part of Romania, and a big area in Yugoslavia.

At first there were tribes of farmers living on the plain by the river Danube, which flows down through the middle of modern Hungary. The Romans invaded the land west of the Danube, but their empire broke up during the fourth century.

Tribes from Germany and the east came swarming in. The land was flat, and lay round a river deep enough for boats, so these big movements of thousands of people were easy.

The Magyar people arrived from Russia at the end of the ninth century A.D. They were herdsmen and fierce raiders. Each tribe had its chief, and the tribes were organized in clans or families. The tribes lost their power as the Magyars settled down, but clans were important for a long time.

The Magyars settled in Transylvania (which is now in Romania) in 896. From then they spread into Hungary. They raided the people around them and were greatly feared. However, when they raided the Germans they were defeated. That was in 955, and afterwards the Magyar leaders thought it wiser to make friends with the Germans. They were converted to the Germans' Roman Catholic faith. On Christmas Day in the year 1000 their overall chief was crowned as Christian king of Hungary, Stephen I.

During the next hundred years Slovakia, Transylvania, and Croatia came under Hungarian rule (these places are now in Czechoslovakia, Romania, and Yugoslavia). The king ruled his big country through his nobles, or magnates, who helped him to defend it. The main threat was from the south-east, where the Turks, Moslems from Asia, had invaded Europe.

The Turks conquered most of Hungary in 1526. The only part they did not control was the western end; this was ruled by Ferdinand of Hapsburg, who claimed the Hungarian throne. He was also ruler of one of the many German-speaking states, Austria. In 1558 he became overlord of all the German states as well.

Ferdinand turned his part of Hungary into a line of fortresses, to keep the Turks away. In 1699 the Turks were defeated altogether. By that time the Hapsburg family had an empire which included Austria and Hungary; it was ruled from the Austrian capital city, Vienna. The most important people in the empire were the Austrians.

The Magyar magnates had to learn the Austrians' German language, and Austrian ways of doing things. During the next 200

53

years they succeeded so well that their own Magyar language went out of fashion. Then in the nineteenth century some Hungarians tried to revive their national language and national identity; they felt that the Austrians were killing both.

The trouble was that not all Hungarians were Magyars. There were Slovaks in Slovakia, Romanians in Transylvania, Croats in Croatia. There were many descendants of German or Austrian solders and settlers, and there were refugees from the Turkish empire. All these people had their own languages, and did not want Magyar forced upon them. They felt about the Magyars as the Magyars felt about the Austrians.

In 1918 the Austrians were defeated in the First World War, and their empire broke up. Hungarian magnates hoped to be able to keep their own big kingdom, but the lands of the Slovaks, Romanians, and Croats were given to new countries. Those lands also had many Magyars, who were now cut off from Hungary.

The new, small Hungary became a republic, which it still is.

PORTUGAL

Portugal is a small country with a long coastline beside the Atlantic Ocean. The climate is damp and temperate. Only the north-east has a harsher climate, like the neighbouring part of Spain.

First, read the piece about Spain, because Portugal was part of Spain until 1139. At that time it was a county belonging to the kingdom of Castile, in central Spain.

The king of Castile was fighting the Moslem rulers of southern Spain; his cousin, Henry of

Burgundy, came to help. Henry was put in charge of Portugal. His son took the title of king in 1139; he ruled over northern and central Portugal, and the rest was gradually won from the Moors.

The Portuguese won more land overseas. From their long coast and many ports they sailed out to make new colonies. During the fifteenth century, in light, tough ships called caravels, they travelled far round the coast of Africa and out to Atlantic islands. After 1500 they founded colonies in the Far East and in South America; the largest of these was Brazil.

Portuguese settlers took with them their Roman Catholic religion and their skills in farming, mining, and forestry. From the colonies great wealth came back to Portugal. The country became a market for goods from all over the world.

During the nineteenth century the royal family, the Braganças, became very unpopular, and there were risings against them. In 1910 there was a revolution, and Portugal became a republic; by that time much of the

54

overseas trade had gone to rival countries. Most of the empire had become independent by 1980. Portugal still governs the Azores, Madeira, and Macao; the first two are Atlantic islands, the third is on the coast of China.

Prince Henry the Navigator. The voyages of exploration he encouraged in the fifteenth century led to the discovery of the sea route to India, and to the vast Portuguese empire.

AUSTRIA

The early people of Austria were Celtic. The Romans conquered them about 58 B.C. The Romans built many forts along the River Danube, which was their frontier.

The Roman empire ended during the fifth century A.D., but Austria was still a frontier state. German tribes invaded it and tried to hold it against enemies from the east; these were Slavs from Bohemia and Magyars from Hungary.

In A.D. 1282 the German king, Rudolf of Hapsburg, made his sons rulers of Austria. The Slav and Magyar rulers never conquered it again, but some Slav and Magyar settlers went on living there under the new German dukes.

The Hapsburg family became extremely powerful. In 1438 they became the hereditary kings of Germany, head of all the small German states. One branch of the family went on to rule Spain and part of Italy; the other branch stayed in Austria, which they made into an important country, with an enormous empire in south-eastern Europe.

This empire was founded in 1526. When the king of the neighbouring countries, Hungary and Bohemia, was killed in battle, Ferdinand of Hapsburg, ruler of Austria, was chosen to succeed him. The empire lasted until 1918; it reached eastwards into Romania, southwards into Yugoslavia, and northwards into Poland. The people of the empire were Germans, Magyars, and Slavs; all these nationalities were to be found living in Vienna, the capital city of Austria. In the Austrian countryside, and the small towns, most of the people were German.

There were many problems as the different parts of the empire wanted more freedom. Many Austrians felt that their German neighbours were their natural allies, while Slavs and Magyars were a source of trouble. German-speaking Austrians were also impressed by the strength and wealth of the newly-united Germany.

In 1914 Austria and Germany were allies in the First World War; they lost, and one of the results of this was that the empire ended. All the Slav and Magyar states which had wanted independence now obtained it.

In 1938 Germany took over Austria. Germany lost a second world war in 1945 and Austria once again became a separate country.

Maria Theresa, Queen of Hungary and of Bohemia, and Archduchess of Austria. Her accession caused the War of the Austrian Succession and, later, was a partial cause of the Seven Years War.

ALBANIA

Albania is a small country with rugged mountains. It has been invaded and divided many times. Various parts of the country have been settled by Greeks, Romans, Bulgarians, Slavs, and Turks; none of these have ever driven the real Albanians out of the mountains.

The Albanians are probably descended from the Illyrians, who lived in this area from at least 1000 B.C. After 620 B.C. the Greeks founded two colonies in Albania. In time, Greek ideas spread out into the surrounding country, which at that time was divided between many rulers. The king of Illyria was the most important; he fought many wars with his powerful neighbour, the king of Macedonia.

The Illyrians and the Macedonians both held parts of Albania. They in turn were conquered by the Romans. After a battle in 168 B.C. the present Albania became part of the Roman empire. The Greek cities became even more important under Roman rule; the Roman empire was divided in A.D. 395, and Albania was included in the Greek-speaking, or eastern, part.

The eastern emperors were never able to keep out invaders. Tribes from Russia and eastern Europe came into the empire, like the Slavs, who attacked Albania. The emperor was unable to defend the Albanian people. The Albanian chieftains had to do it themselves. They built fortified towns, and used their own armies. Before long, they were the real rulers of the country, but as well as fighting the Slavs, they fought each other.

The Turks, from Asia, were the next invaders. These were not warlike tribesmen but professional soldiers. To defeat them, the chiefs had to unite, and they could not do it.

The Turks became overlords of Albania after 1390. There were rebellions against them, especially under the soldier George Kastriote Skanderbeg, but the Turks had complete control by 1506. They ruled Albania until 1912. They brought in the Moslem religion, which became the faith of most Albanians.

When Turkish rule ended the Albanians wanted one independent country for all the people who spoke the Albanian language. They found it hard to convince other countries that they were a nation, with a language and a culture of their own.

The Albanians declared themselves independent in 1912. There was still disagreement between different groups and political parties, as there had been between the medieval chiefs. There were also more invasions, especially during the First World War of 1914–18.

Albania was invaded again, by Italy, and occupied from 1939 until 1944. After the occupation ended the country became independent, with a communist government.

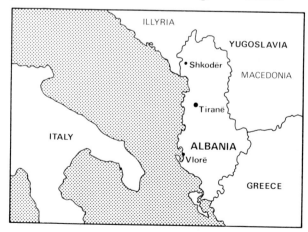

ICELAND

Iceland is a large island in the north Atlantic Ocean. Most of it is made up of mountains (of which many are volcanoes) and vast areas of ice and volcanic larva. Nearly all the towns and villages are near the coast.

The first villages were founded by Vikings — men who came by sea from Norway in about A.D. 874. Vikings were soldiers, pirates, traders, and explorers. They were fierce, practical, and very tough. They brought groups of settlers; some settlers came from Norway and some from Viking colonies in Ireland, Scotland, and the Isle of Man.

For a long time the Icelanders ruled themselves. In 1264 they agreed to be ruled by Norway. When Norway was taken over by Denmark in 1537, so was Iceland.

Iceland was always a difficult country to live in. The land and the climate made farming very hard. The people depended on the sea, for fishing and shipping.

During the Second World War (1939 – 45) Iceland was an American military base. This brought some prosperity, and in 1944 the Icelanders declared themselves independent of Denmark. However, they are still very like the people of Denmark and Norway in their language and way of life.

Iceland owes its existence entirely to volcanic action. Here is the volcano of Hekla in eruption.

GIBRALTAR

The name 'Gibraltar' comes from Gebel Tarik, which means the Rock of Tarik. Tarik was an African warrior who landed on this rocky peninsula, off the south coast of Spain, in 711. His followers set up an African Moslem kingdom in southern Spain. Gibraltar was part of that kingdom until the Spaniards took it in 1462. In 1713 Gibraltar became a British colony, which it still is. Most of the people are of Spanish or Portuguese descent; some are descended from Italian merchants and sailors. Both English and Spanish are spoken. Gibraltar was important because it guarded the strait at the entrance to the Mediterranean Sea. It is still a military base, which is where most of the people work. (See map of Spain.)

SAN MARINO

San Marino is a very small republic, only 24 square miles (61 square kilometres). It lies in the Apennine mountains in Italy. San Marino has existed since before A.D. 400. At that time, there were many tiny states in Italy, with Italian-speaking people. When the others joined the new, united kingdom of Italy in 1861–70, San Marino chose to remain as an independent town. (See map of Italy.)

Two views of Gibraltar. This rocky eminence at the southern tip of Spain has been a British possession since 1713.

Glossary

Celt: An ancient people of north-western Europe of whom Irish, Welsh, and Bretons are the main descendants.

Catholic: A member of the Roman Catholic church.

First World War 1914–18: A war between Britain, France, Russia and others, against Germany, Austro-Hungary, Bulgaria, and others.

Franks: An ancient Germanic people who conquered France about A.D. 500.

Illyria: An ancient country on the east Adriatic coast.

Magyars: A people who originated in the area of modern Hungary.

Middle Ages: The period covering the fifth to fourteenth centuries in Europe.

Normans: A branch of the Vikings who in the tenth century A.D. conquered Normandy and settled there. In the eleventh century they conquered Britain.

Moslems: Members of the church founded in Arabia in the seventh century A.D., who invaded and settled in southern Spain and most of the Balkans.

Orthodox church: A Christian church of those countries in the Eastern Roman Empire and in a few other countries of eastern Europe.

Protestant church: A Christian church which separated from the Roman Catholic Church in the sixteenth century.

Roman Catholic church: A Christian church which accepts the Bishop of Rome (the Pope) as its supreme head.

Roman empire: The empire established by the Romans in the first century B.C. It eventually covered all the countries of the Mediterranean and all Europe up to the Rhine and Danube. At the end of the fourth century A.D. it was divided into Western and Eastern Empires. The Western Empire ended in 476 A.D. The Eastern Empire, ruled from Byzantium (Constantinople) lasted until the fifteenth century.

Romans: In this book the word always refers to the Roman empire, its armies, and its settlers.

Second World War 1939–45: A war between Britain and France (and later U.S.A. and Russia) against Germany, Italy, Japan and others.

Slavs: A race of peoples widely spread over eastern, southern, and central Europe including Russians, Bulgars, Serbs, Croats, Slovenes, Poles, Czechs, Moravians, and Slovaks.

Thrace: An ancient region in the Balkan Peninsula roughly corresponding to modern Bulgaria, Greece, and European Turkey.

Turks: Moslem invaders from Turkey who colonized the Balkans and Greece between the fifteenth and early twentieth centuries.

Vikings: Scandinavian sea-raiders (and later settlers) upon the coasts of north-west Europe between the eighth and tenth centuries A.D.

Index

Africa 4, 49, 54, 58
Albania 25, 38, 58
Alderney 52
Alemanni 30
Andorra 26
Angles 44–7
Anjou 21
Antwerp 7
Aquitaine 21
Arabs 47
Aragon 5
Arcadia 38
Argos 38
Asturias 4
Athens 38
Attica 38
Austria 7, 14, 18, 53–4, 56
Azores 11, 55

Balearic Islands 6
Basques 4, 6
Bavaria 30, 36
Belgium 6–8, 23
Bogomils 25
Bohemia 36, 56
Bosnia-Hercogovina 24
Brazil 54 (see also Peoples and Nations
    of The Americas)
Britain 10; see also United Kingdom
Brittany 21
Bruges 7
Bulgaria 24, 28, 38
Burgundy 20, 42
Byzantium 24, 29, 38

Cadiz 4
Carthaginians 4, 49
Castile 4, 54
Catholic Church, see Orthodox church;
    Roman Catholic church
Celts 6, 10, 20, 23, 42, 44–7, 56
Channel Islands 52
Christians 4, 6, 10, 20, 32, 44, 49, 56;
    see also Orthodox church; Roman
    Catholic church
Comino 47
Connaught 10
Constantinople 24, 38
Corinth 38
Corsica 23
Cracow 17

Crete 38
Croatia 24, 53–4
Cyprus 32
Czechoslovakia 36–7, 53

Dacia 34
Dalmatia 24
Denmark 19–20, 26, 28, 31, 34, 44, 47,
    50–51, 58
Dorians 38
Dublin 10
Dutch, see Holland

East Germany, see Germany
Eire, see Ireland
empires
    Austrian and Austro-Hungarian 18,
    23, 24, 25, 36, 53–4, 56
    British 33, 47, 49, 60
    Danish 47
    Dutch 15–16
    Frankish 20, 23, 30–31
    French 49
    German 24, 31
    Greek 12, 32, 38
    Macedonian 28
    Portuguese 54–5
    Roman, see Roman empire
    Spanish 5, 15
    Turkish 25, 29–30, 33, 39–40, 53–4,
    58
England, see United Kingdom
Etruscans 12

Faeroes 19, 20, 34, 50–51
Finland 8, 27–8
Flanders 7
Flemings 8
Florence 14
France 7–8, 14, 16, 20–23, 30, 47,
    49, 52
Franks 6–7, 15, 20, 30
Friesians 15, 30

Gauls 20
Genoa 14
Germany 7, 9, 16, 17, 18–19, 20, 27,
    30, 30–32, 36–37, 42, 44, 50–51,
    53–54, 56
Ghent 7
Gibraltar 60

Goths 13
Gotland 26
Gozo 49
Granada 5
Great Britain, see United Kingdom
Greater Moravia 36
Greece 4, 12, 24, 32, 38–40, 58
Greenland 51
Guernsey 52

Holland 7–8, 15–16, 23
Hungary 34, 36, 53–4, 56

Ibiza 6
Iceland 19, 20, 50–51, 58
Illyrians 24, 38, 58
Illyricum 24
India 47 (see also Peoples and Nations of
    Asia)
Ireland 10–11, 44, 47, 58
Isle of Man 47, 51, 58
Istanbul (Byzantium, Constantinople)
    24, 29
Italy 12–14, 58, 60; see also Roman
    empire

Jersey 52
Jutes 44–7

Kingdom of the Serbs, Croats, and
    Slovenes 25

languages
    Arabic 49
    Basque 4
    Catalan 26
    Czech 36
    Dutch 6
    English 60
    French 6, 23, 26, 42, 47, 49
    Gaelic 47
    Germanic 9, 15, 18, 23, 24, 30, 31,
    42
    Greek 24, 28–9, 38, 40
    Italian 42, 60
    Latin 12, 34, 47
    Letzeburgesch 23
    Magyar 54
    Maltese 49
    Monégasque 49
    Romansch 42

Scandinavian (Norse) 19, 47
Serbo-Croat 24
Sicilian 49
Slovene 24, 29
Spanish 26, 60
Welsh 47
Lapps 8, 9, 19
Leinster 10
Liechtenstein 9
Liège 47
Lithuania 18
Lombards 13
Low Countries 7; see also Belgium;
  Holland
Lusitanians 4
Luxembourg 23

Macao 55
Macedonia 24, 28–30, 38, 40, 58
Madeira 55
Magyars 31, 34–5, 36–7, 53, 56
Majorca 6
Manx 47
Milan 14
Minorca 6
Moldavia 34
Malta 49
Monaco 49
Mongols 18
Montenegro 25
Moors 4–5, 54
Moravia 36
Moriscos 4
Moslems 4; see also Moors
Mozarabs 4
Mudejars 4
Munster 10

Navarre 5
Netherlands, see Holland
Normans 14, 20, 47
Northern Ireland, see Ireland; United
  Kingdom
Norway 19, 20, 28, 34, 47, 50–51, 58

Oland 26
Orthodox church 24, 25, 29, 32, 34, 36,
  38, 40

Pakistan 47 (see also Peoples and
  Nations of Asia)
Phoenicians 4
Picts 44–7
Pisa 14
Poland 17–19, 56
Popes 13–14, 18
Portugal 4, 11, 54–5, 60
Protestantism 11, 15, 20, 22, 27, 31,
  34–5, 42, 47, 51
Provence 20
Prussia 18, 31–2

Reformation 15, 22, 31, 42
religions
  Bogomil 24
  Christianity 4, 6, 11, 15, 24, 31, 36;
  see also Orthodox church;
  Protestantism; Roman Catholic church
  Islam 4–6, 29, 34, 54, 58, 60
  Scandinavian 49
Roman Catholic church 4–6, 11, 13,
  17–18, 21–2, 23, 31, 34–5, 36, 38,
  42, 53, 54
Roman empire 4, 6, 12–13, 20, 23, 24,
  28, 31, 32, 34, 36, 38, 42, 44, 49,
  53, 56, 58
Romania 34–5, 38, 53–4, 56
Russia 8–9, 18–19, 26, 28, 30, 35, 36,
  53, 58 (see also Peoples and Nations of
  Asia)

Samnites 12
San Marino 60
Sardinia 12
Sark 52
Savoy 42
Saxons 30, 44–7
Scandinavians, see Denmark; Norway;
  Sweden

Scotland 11, 58; see also United
  Kingdom
Serbia 24
Sicily 12, 49
Silesia 17
Slavs 17, 24, 29, 31, 36–7, 38, 58
Slovakia 36, 53–4
Slovenia 24
Spain 4–6, 7, 14, 15, 54, 58
Sparta 38
Spitsbergen 19
Svear people 26
Sweden 8, 19–20, 26–8, 50
Switzerland 42

Tartars 18
Thebes 38
Thessaly 38
Thracians 24, 28, 34
Thuringians 30
Transylvania 34–5, 53–4
Turkey 25, 29, 33, 34, 39–40, 53–4, 58
  (see also Peoples and Nations of Asia)

Ulster 10
United Kingdom 10–11, 44–7, 52
United States of America 11, 59 (see
  also People and Nations of The
  Americas)

Vaduz 9
Vatican City 14
Venice 14
Vikings 6, 10, 19–20, 20, 26–7, 34, 47,
  50, 51, 58
Vlachs 38

Wales, see United Kingdom
Wallachia 34
Walloons 8
West Germany, see Germany
West Indies 47

Yugoslavia 24, 38, 40, 53, 56

PICTURE ACKNOWLEDGEMENTS

Austrian Institute 57; Author 22, 25, 39, 46, 50/51; Belgian Embassy 6; Bodleian Library 12, 13, 16, 21, 32, 45; Bulgarian Cultural Institute 28, 29; Cedok (London) Ltd 37; Cyprus High Commission 33; Embassy of Federal Republic of Germany 30, 31; Embassy of Iceland 59; Finnish Tourist Board 9; Gibraltar Govt Tourist Office 60, 61; Mary Evans Picture Libary 35, 48; National Library of Ireland 10, 11; National Tourist Organization of Greece 41; Patrimonie des Musees Royaux des Beaux-Arts, Brussels 7; Portuguese National Tourist Office 55; Rijksmuseum-Stichting, Amsterdam 14; Royal Netherlands Embassy 15; Royal Norwegian Embassy 21; Societe Jersiase 52; Spanish National Tourist Office 5; Swedish Institute 26, 26/7; Swiss National Tourist Office 43; Young Library 40.